ROYA MARSH

dayliGht

LaQuann Dawson

Roya Marsh, a Bronx, New York, native, is a nationally recognized poet, performer, educator, and activist. She is the Poet in Residence at Urban Word NYC, and she works feverishly toward LGBTQIA justice and dismantling white supremacy. Marsh's work has been featured on NBC, BET, Button Poetry, Write About Now Poetry, Def Jam's All Def Digital, and *Lexus Verses and Flow*, and in *Poetry* magazine, *Flypaper Magazine*, *Frontier Poetry*, *The Village Voice*, *Nylon*, *HuffPost*, and *The BreakBeat Poets Volume 2: Black Girl Magic* (2018).

daylight

daylight

daylight

ROYA MARSH

MCD × FSG Originals

Farrar, Straus and Giroux [*New York*]

MCD × FSG Originals
Farrar, Straus and Giroux
120 Broadway, New York 10271

Printed in the United States of America
First edition, 2020

Library of Congress Cataloging-in-Publication Data
Names: Marsh, Roya, 1988– author.
Title: dayliGht / Roya Marsh.
Description: First edition. | New York : MCD × FSG Originals/
Farrar, Straus and Giroux, 2020.
Identifiers: LCCN 2019046777 | ISBN 9780374538897
(hardcover)
Subjects: LCSH: Women, Black—Poetry. | LCGFT: Poetry.
Classification: LCC PS3613.A76987 D39 2020 | DDC 811/.6—
dc23
LC record available at https://lccn.loc.gov/2019046777

Designed by Richard Oriolo

10 9 8 7 6 5 4 3 2 1

For

Geraldine,

Gayla,

and

Glynis

Geraldine, Grandma

Gayla, Ma

Glynis, Aunty

contents

A NOTE FROM THE AUTHOR:
ON BLACK BUTCH REPRESENTATION IN *DAYLIGHT* xiii

in broad dayliGht black girls look ghost 4

in broad dayliGht black descendants look gall 6

in broad dayliGht bruised black girls look goals 8

in broad dayliGht black girls look gat 11

in broad dayliGht black activists look gunshot 14

in broad dayliGht black girls look gat II 15

in broad dayliGht black moms look grieving 19

in broad dayliGht black aunties with no man look damn good 21

in broad dayliGht black saviors look grandma 23

in broad dayliGht black daughters look gossip 25

in broad dayliGht suicidal black girls look guilty 27

in broad dayliGht black girls look grave 29

in broad dayliGht battered black women look grazed 30

in broad dayliGht black girls look grim 32

in broad dayliGht black dykes look ground 34

in broad dayliGht kinky black girls look g-spot 36

in broad dayliGht black daughters look greedy 37

in broad dayliGht black girls look gleeful 38

in broad dayliGht black dykes look good enough to fuck 39

in broad dayliGht black dykes look glow 43

in broad dayliGht black catcalled dykes look grumpy 44

in broad dayliGht black women look grouchy 46

in broad dayliGht black bipolar girls look grimy 48

in broad dayliGht black victims looked gagged 50

homage to dyke girls with gap-tooth smiles 56

in broad dayliGht black mfa candidates look glamorous 58

in broad dayliGht black dykes look go 60

in broad dayliGht black sisters look glass 62

in broad dayliGht black dykes look gomorrah 65

in broad dayliGht black queer femmes look gala 68

in broad dayliGht black stars look like gyrochronology 69

in broad dayliGht black dykes look grilled 72

in broad dayliGht black abuse victims look gone 75

in broad dayliGht black thrivers look growth 80

in broad dayliGht black moms look swollen gland 81

in broad dayliGht black lovers look guest 84

what are the conditions of your freedom? 88

ACKNOWLEDGMENTS 91

a note from the author:
On Black Butch Representation in *dayliGht*

REPRESENTATION MATTERS. I was eight years old the first time I saw a representation of someone *like me*. It was 1996, when Queen Latifah made her big-screen debut as Cleopatra "Cleo" Sims in F. Gary Gray's *Set It Off.* It meant everything to me to see a Black woman living her life openly gay; openly masc presenting; with cornrows, baggy jeans, plaid shirts, and big breasts. I was twenty-eight years old when Lena Waithe became the first African American woman to take home an Emmy award for her work on Aziz Ansari's *Master of None*. The episode for which she won the award chronicles the

Roya

coming-out story of Waithe's character, Denise. These are representations that have buoyed and emboldened me.

Children who are sexually assaulted are reborn into fire. There's always a trail of smoke. There's always a pile of ash. Some folks believe these assaults might sway our sexuality. Sometimes, this is true. But it's not always the case. At least, it wasn't for me. Both trauma and the attendant coping mechanisms we devise to live with trauma manifest in countless ways—it all depends on the host upon which our traumas feed.

I knew who I was and who I was going to be well before I was assaulted. I was eight years old when I knew I was going to love women romantically. Even at that age I knew what desire looked like. The youngest of eight children, I was hypersexualized by proximity. Sex was everywhere. Yet, my exposure to sex was limited to heteronormative behaviors and depictions.

I knew I was "different." My family knew I was "different." But homosexuality wasn't something that was prevalent, much less discussed, in my family. Anything outside the heteronorm was passed off as "funny." My sexuality was either completely disregarded or couched in homophobic epithets. From the moment I was able to dress myself, I wore windbreakers and superhero T-shirts. Dresses, barrettes, and the like were never my thing, but I wasn't in charge of my hair just yet. In overalls, I was "tomboy" passing.

Experiencing an assault in my childhood made me vulnerable to assault in my teenage years. Later, seeking support, I found brick walls instead. To this day, I'm met with ignorance when I raise the subject with those closest to me. Some folks just can't fathom any hetero-predator wanting a girl like me. Some folks just can't fathom a woman like me having sex appeal to a man eager to conquer.

Most days my femininity is catcalled into existence. I'm considered just woman enough—enough to fuck into a condition the world will accept. I know representation isn't a cure, but it's a start. I fear violence against my community will continue to go unabated unless we continue to tell our stories and fight for a wider understanding of the full spectrum of sexuality and gender.

When I see Cleo, I see myself—even if I also see a level of toxic masculinity and an objectification of women in her character that I struggle against. In Cleo, I see wit. I see strength. I see pride (to a fault). And I see a woman with a drive to become utterly *unfuckwithable*. When I see Denise, I see myself. I see a woman living her best lesbian life; dealing with the ebb and flow of others' perceptions.

SINCE THE RISE OF THE #MeToo movement, I have longed (perhaps, selfishly enough) to see women who look like me come forward. Of course, that's not to say that I want to see us as victims. Rather, I want the world to know that there isn't only one type of victim. I'm calling us to the front because I know we exist—women, like me, trapped in yet another closet. I don't see our stories represented often enough. I want the Google image results for search terms like "strong Black woman" and "bad bitch" to look like us, too—the Masculine of Center (MoC) woman, the butch, the colored dyke, the survivor who struggles with forgiveness. I am forever indebted to those writers and artists who've showcased these characters and narratives—to Audre Lorde, and Barbara Smith, and Anita Cornwell, and Alice Dunbar-Nelson, and June Jordan, and countless others. It is my hope to add an ember to the flames they've lit.

We often forget the wonders of fire. There may be smoke at the start and ash at the end, but always in its wake lies evidence of the work done to light the way.

dayliGht

BLACK BLACK BLACK BLACK BLACK BLACK BLACK BLACK
BLACK BLACK BLACK BLACK BLACK BLACK BLACK BLACK
BLACK BLACK BLACK BLACK BLACK BLACK BLACK BLACK
BLACK BLACK BLACK BLACK BLACK BLACK BLACK BLACK
BLACK BLACK BLACK BLACK BLACK BLACK BLACK BLACK
BLACK BLACK BLACK BLACK BLACK BLACK BLACK BLACK
BLACK BLACK BLACK BLACK BLACK BLACK BLACK BLACK
BLACK BLACK BLACK BLACK BLACK BLACK BLACK BLACK
BLACK BLACK BLACK BLACK BLACK BLACK BLACK BLACK
BLACK BLACK BLACK BLACK BLACK BLACK BLACK BLACK
BLACK BLACK BLACK BLACK BLACK BLACK BLACK BLACK
BLACK BLACK BLACK BLACK BLACK BLACK BLACK BLACK
BLACK BLACK BLACK BLACK BLACK BLACK BLACK BLACK
BLACK BLACK BLACK BLACK BLACK BLACK BLACK BLACK
BLACK BLACK BLACK BLACK BLACK BLACK BLACK BLACK
BLACK BLACK BLACK BLACK BLACK BLACK BLACK BLACK
BLACK BLACK BLACK BLACK BLACK BLACK BLACK BLACK
BLACK BLACK BLACK BLACK BLACK BLACK BLACK BLACK
BLACK BLACK BLACK BLACK BLACK BLACK BLACK BLACK
BLACK BLACK BLACK BLACK BLACK BLACK BLACK BLACK
BLACK BLACK BLACK BLACK BLACK BLACK BLACK BLACK
BLACK BLACK BLACK BLACK BLACK BLACK BLACK BLACK
BLACK BLACK BLACK BLACK BLACK BLACK BLACK BLACK
BLACK BLACK BLACK BLACK BLACK BLACK BLACK BLACK
BLACK BLACK BLACK BLACK BLACK BLACK BLACK BLACK
BLACK BLACK BLACK BLACK BLACK BLACK BLACK BLACK
BLACK BLACK BLACK BLACK BLACK BLACK BLACK BLACK
BLACK BLACK BLACK BLACK BLACK BLACK BLACK BLACK
BLACK BLACK BLACK BLACK BLACK BLACK BLACK BLACK
BLACK BLACK BLACK BLACK BLACK BLACK BLACK BLACK
BLACK BLACK BLACK BLACK BLACK BLACK BLACK BLACK
BLACK BLACK BLACK BLACK BLACK BLACK BLACK BLACK
BLACK BLACK BLACK BLACK BLACK BLACK BLACK BLACK
BLACK BLACK BLACK BLACK BLACK BLACK BLACK BLACK
BLACK BLACK BLACK BLACK BLACK BLACK BLACK BLACK
BLACK BLACK BLACK BLACK BLACK BLACK BLACK BLACK

in broad dayliGht black girls look ghost

Carefully, i arrange my disguise. It has been designed not to stand out . . . i decide to look like a poor Black woman.
—ASSATA SHAKUR

i'm good with my tongue.
it makes me most visible.
with a shut mouth I'm a good dresser.
    a flapping tongue makes me:
            sexy
        well learned
        a conquest

my voice is more pronounced than my skin tone
and i need to know why
i track down my ancestry through DNA
i track down someone with *my* last name
she tell me it's hers
she white
says it's funny how I'm black
i say, "ha-ha"
results say i'm hers
in history
in old law
in old English

say her great greats

owned my greatest

on this soil.

"wow," she say

and i hold my tongue. tight. between molars.

'til it bloody and useless

'til i can't speak

'til she don't see me

and swallow back the blood i ain't ask for in the first place

in broad dayliGht black descendants look gall

a saturday

betwixt the chin-high grass

hot enough to scald a lizard

beneath the mason dixon

a single home in a field of trailers

the big house

we dancing

the floorboards creak

the howl of a billion souls unfree

the record spins

the beat repeats

you still away,

steal away

heavenward

where your grands' grands will belong to no one

'cept themselves

steal away to own your own body

what is it about learning you have a body that makes
   having a body so damn complicated?

joy is an impossible thing to remember

to forget

to know yourself as your own, but still a descendant of theft

joy to be free in vain

as a result of someone else's captivity

two black women

egos the top rung of a ladder

trapped in the body of a ditch

but we wobble

atop a warehouse of stolen caskets

the dance floor shimmys back

sayin' g'head girl, this joy is yours

in broad dayliGht bruised black girls look goals*

an erasure for emily b. and tonie nicole wells

One and then the two

Two and then the three

Three and then the four

Then you gotta . . . (LEAVE)

Then you gotta . . .

Then you gotta . . .

Yo, ████████████████ when I come through

███████████████████████ man

It's not even funny, ███████████

██ chokehold's too tight

██ left looks too right

███████████████

These bitches can't █████

Look, look, they hearts racing, ██████████

███████████████ ████████████████

In the presence of the man

Your future █████████ your past ███████████

  the man

You █████████

* lyrics from fabolous's "breathe."

One and then the two

Two and then the three

Three and then the four

Then you gotta . . .

Then you gotta . . .

Then you gotta . . .

LEAVE!

what the world gon' say 'bout a single mother?

same shit they say 'bout a battered one.

q. what she do to make him go off

a. stay

fight. tooth 'n' nail. call daddy.

when yo' baby daddy forget he not yo' daddy.

when your whole relationship been a game of dress-up

& the costumes come off

in front the camera. in front the world.

and you live long enough to be hashtagged into fault

defense of the abusive black rapper

stretches longer than turkey day leftovers

& you surplus, crumbs from the dust of *woman* and *color*.

black bitch.

gold digger.

how dare you save yourself.

we told you, die.

so we could RIP you, sis.

look at tonie,

gone

from *giving us life* on theshaderoom

to *dead on the basement floor.*

barry gets life, but not her.

devalued. dumb. doomed.

y'know, i do wanna see both sides.

rip entry & exit wound.

repent and reform.

i'll wait and will and work

'til then . . .

"I got a bullet with your [fame] on it."

one and then the two

in broad dayliGht black girls look gat

a found poem from Facebook comments

March 24 at 1:19 p.m.

Why do you have a gun?

Comments:

Because I was expected to own a rifle where I grew up.

Why not to protect another life in a dire situation against one's own ideals and morality?

(drake voice) maybe one day? Maybe one day

Because white people are crazy

Because it's my right, I've been victim of an unexpected home invasion after a vacation that left me shot & I refuse to get another gunshot wound.

I know people that happen to be the same color as me are dumb. I don't need/have one. I'm just saying that gun control starts within oneself. If you don't need it for work or survival or hunting, you don't need one at all.

███████ Keywords here are need & survival.

Is that all?

███████ Varmints

███████ Looney tunes . . . lol we. Laughed every time Elmer Fudd tried to shoot the wabbit knowing he never would. We grow up and see: That's not the actual result

███████ To blow that bitch if I need to protect myself.

███████ Growing up, they were commonplace. Used to shoot cans in the desert. Now, I can't have one. Too much of a risk to myself. But you know, a good pellet rifle is just fine for shooting cans these days. If I wanna go target shooting, I can go to the range and pick whatever rediculous cartoon boomstick I want.

███████ My great-grandfather was murdered over a quarter. My younger brother was murdered over nothing. People will try to kill you before you even think about fighting them. And I have two children i must protect.

Simple answer, i can't trust people.

█████ Because its 2018 and i'm black, plus my family hunts

in broad dayliGht black activists look gunshot

In a conversation about the fiftieth anniversary of MLK Jr.'s
assassination my father says,
"They don't kill no one important in the U.S. no mo'."

and how easy he forgets.
how a happy home dies in a snapshot.
how language is loaded.
how i was raised loaded for bear.
how he been a half-cocked father.
how my brother got swallowed by a barrel.
how that's his own forgotten blood not even 10 years
gone.
how gaping the vacancy beside my mother at his funeral.
how he go exit wound whenever he see fit.
how he sweat bullets when we question his absence.
how I'm a short-tempered straight shooter triggered to go
ballistic.
how he return ready w/ silencer anytime i shoot off my
mouth.
how he the reason I ain't never been no stranger to the
business end of a gun.
how he ain't never mean no harm, he just shooting the
breeze.

in broad dayliGht black girls look gat II

a found poem from Facebook comments

March 28 at 3:18 p.m.

Why don't you have a gun?

Comments:

Because I'm afraid I would use it.

what said. Also my cousin
murdered in cold blood by her my more than 2 cents
take em away from everyone, including the mofo
government. then we b gud

^ precisely.

Strapped

Because I don't want to take
another person's life.

You don't HAVE to kill anyone just
because you have a gun . . .

I was raised around guns, and more than once had a need to use them. My father once told me that you should never pull a gun unless you intend to use it. Well, he ended up getting murdered and I decided to not to live the kind of life that made me feel like I needed to use that kind of force to keep myself safe. I don't have a gun because I don't ever want to shoot someone.

Because I don't trust myself not to use it.

Cause I've been lucky enough to not have to use/need one

Because I was planning on using it the last time I checked myself into a mental hospital.

Because with my luck an attacker would take it from me and use it on me. Why arm the little mother effers? #igotknees

Because I don't want to get shot

Because it cost to much to have and maintain legally.

It's much easier to get one off the street and just pay for the piece not worrying about a license, background checks, or safety classes.

Something's wrong with this picture . . . SMH

█████ Because I come from a family of suicide. Because my grandfather committed suicide with a shotgun. Because I have told my doctors about my own suicidal thoughts. Because with this information, they would not let me have one.

█████ Because it is more likely to hurt someone close to my heart than to protect them.

█████ Taking classes soon like saturday soon. To legally own

█████ Becuz I have more than one

█████ Honestly—it's not something that ever occurred to me to consider.

█████ Because I have the distinct privilege not to live in the kind of fear that requires it. I've never felt the need for it.

█████ 1 they kill niggas for toy guns

2 my suicidal ideation + gun = . . .

3 I have 3 kids they get into more shit than I ever thought kids could . . . See more

█████ Because I can't think of a place I could hide it, that my kids couldn't find it.

█████ Sold them all when I retired.

█████ Because I don't have enough balance to hold it and would probably get taken off my feet by the kickback.

█████ I have a gun. It has 66 bullets. Demons are afraid it and abusers don't know how to use it properly.

█████ Because I have a pen

█████ They don't block bullets and therefore do not protect anyone.

in broad dayliGht black moms look grieving

a poem in response to Facebook comments

they have made hell

a home, on earth.

camera captures breath.

concrete captures body.

this is NOTHING

new.

yanking the limbs of breathless,

bleeding bodies behind backs.

i, too, yell commands to the deceased

the hole(y),

they seldom respond accordingly.

that is not a crime—

the yelling or the dying.

the shooting—that is the sin.

my mother says,

if you have a gun

you'll shoot a gun.

so, i don't have a gun

i think . . .

if you have a pen

you will shoot a pen.

i never thought a bullet
could write this many poems.
they do not sweat
when *they* grab *their* gun.
i do not sweat
when i grab my pen.

the difference is in our bullets

in broad dayliGht black aunties with no man look damn good

"Cruisin'," Smokey Robinson plays for Glynis

the genes in my family are strong. everybody got a
doppelganger. at least 10 years their senior
take my sister, sam. got my mama whole face 33 years
later. look like my brother spit my nephew zay right out
his left nut. and he aint even his boy. bricyn make it seem
like akil was born twice. all the way up to the autism. me,
i lent my likeness to joe//in more ways than one. he got my
gap-tooth'd smile
the twinkle in my eye & the twinkle in his
wrist too.

me, i look so much like my aunty glynis, in my
gramma's last years there wasn't even a chance she'd
tell us apart. aunty say i'm her bonus daughter. in
secret. out of wedlock. say she let my mama borrow
me on account of what they say about women with kids
but no man.

no man. i ain't never seen her with no man.

baby daddy dead.
husband dead.
dead, years before my mama even thought of havin' a
baby girl.

aunty got a daughter of her own tho. a pretty brown-
skin thang with a gap like the best of us and eyes
light something like Smokey Robinson.
& ain't no man aunty love more than
light-eyed smokey.

no man.

i seen her eyes light
up at his tender pitch. a perfect kind of soft and bright.
i ain't saying she never longed for a loving touch. that she
never rolled over to an empty bedside
and wept a river of lonely.
i'm saying she make flying solo look like a drop-
top drive down the pacific coast.
i'm sayin i ain't never felt more felt than when watchin' her
live out her every dream with a passport in one palm and
unlimited freedom in the other.

You're gonna fly away, glad you're goin' my way
I love it when we're cruisin' together

in broad dayliGht black saviors look grandma

or, i think i built that wall myself
or, my grandmother would never play craps

i ain't never liked gambling. my grandmother's last
hoorah was at a casino in atlantic city. she could talk then.
i remember because she called home in a panicked haze
when the jackpot lights were all too much and she forgot
the bus that took her there was the same bus that would
take her back. my family took a gamble when putting
her in a nursing home. she could talk then. i remember
because she hated that place and was of course fed up with
the incompetence of those in power. she saw the country
take a gamble on its first black president. the best eight
years of my life. the last eight years of hers. she was mute
for years before the end. i remember because she never
wished me a happy 21st. or maybe she did, but i wasn't
close enough to hear it. i guess i forgot how to listen. i
forgot how to talk to someone who couldn't talk back.
months before she died this country took a gamble on red.
she couldn't talk no more. i hadn't been listening anyway.
but i bet she had a few choice words for what'd make
this country great. for the first time. he been ruining this
country for 457 days. she been gone for 251 days. i been
going double or nothing with my sanity at stake. like going

broke gon' fix anything. i was gon' write this to her but i keep telling myself she'll never hear it. i think i built that wall myself.

in broad dayliGht black daughters look gossip

No one in my church knows my father
but I carry his name. head bowed
in prayer. in shame. in offering
empty palms turned up at the altar.
i am nothing more than his daughter
begging another man i have never seen.
for mercy. for love. for saving.
there is never a good enough lie to tell.
the truth is always gone.
i am a lonely audience while
the choir hums & the congregation peers over their
shoulder. they say neighbor
and the air whispers lonely. the whispers whisper
come forth. no one whispers forgive. so i don't.
i just carry my void on my shoulders. at the dance. on
paper. on my tithes. on my wedding day.
on my smile.
everyone says that's my best feature. says it lights up a
room. could light up the sky.
i think that kind of metaphor is what killed christ.
i was born and named and left.
this smile was born with a window
all my sacred keeps slippin' right through.
& i just let it. ain't no sense in chasing what ain't tryna be
caught,

that goes for liquors.

that goes for lovers.

that goes for leavers.

Remember,

no one in my church knows my father

they just know his name.

and pray my strength in His name.

But this name

is mine & all its history.

this smile

is mine & all its fissures.

what comes and goes from my mouth will have been crafted of my own legend.

& who i choose to worship is the one facing me in the mirror

of my own altar.

in broad dayligGht suicidal black girls look guilty

cross-examining myself while on trial after my third failed suicide attempt:

Please state your name for the record. ██████. You were working as a poet, activist, and educator for a non-profit at the time of the assault, is that correct? Yes. Is it true that your work doesn't offer you a real chance to clock out? Yes. Is it true that you have never refused to work overtime? My job is to be as real as possible. You can not turn that off. Your family craves more attention than they are owed, correct? . . . They are often the last on your list of priorities, isn't that right? No. What of the dead? . . . Your grandmother died on your birthday, is that correct? Yes. How often did you spend time with her? As much as I could, I swear. Is it true that you spent your entire summer writing poems and traveling to perform? No. Well, yes, but not entirely. Is it yes or no, Ms. ████? I, I—I don't know. I was with her every chance I could be. And you only came in second place? Was it worth it? . . . Again, what of the dead? Not just your grandmother, but what of your brother? What of the one with no gun? What of the one with mental illness? Dead. All dead. What did you do for them? How do you feel knowing you're still breathing? Would you rather trade places with the deceased? Withdrawn. Of course you would.

Objection. Can you . . . ? Can you object? You object-ify your sanity on a daily basis because you have yet to learn a better way to survive. Sometimes wanting to die and trying to are the only reminders that you are still alive. Ms. █████, you are still alive.

In direct examination, you stated that you are in control, is that correct? Yes. But you failed. You are a failure. That's not a question. What do you know of control? You are a failure that fails at failing. That's not a question. Why were you unsuccessful? What went wrong? Where are you now? What of the body? Where is the body? Where is your body, Ms. █████?

You wanna know what I did with the body? What is a body, anyway? Known only because someone called it so. Without my consent. Awarded me this trophy. Covered in fingerprints, dust & grime. The body should be on trial. Fuck, the body is a trial. My memory, a field of landmines. I blink and everything I have tried to forget blows up in my face. The shrapnel, that is where I exist. In the rations of everything that has happened to me. Not in a body. So, I tried to get rid of it. Use it against itself. If you look hard enough down the throat of a bottle. You'll find it. Lying, almost lifeless, somewhere between death and freedom.

in broad dayliGht black girls look grave

name one thing you can't find buried in the core of a black
woman . . .
I'll wait . . .

The scariest thing is the way we hate ourselves. How we are taught this. How we oblige. Where we let them burrow falsehoods into our notion of self-love and sow a name on it—watch it grow. And watch us reap. And watch us weep. No cedarwood box. Our living corpse casket enough. Mummified in misogynoir. A dark place to hide the weight of the world. They gon' throw dirt on our name. They gon' throw dirt on us. Each grain of soil another tale they told. Another foot dug. Deep. Deeper. Sorry. Silent. Sister. Small. Sexy. Slut. Solemn. Sick. Sadness. Sanity. Sinner. Sinking. You clawing your way out. Or trying. They keep on shoveling.

Who knew SOS meant save ourselves.

in broad dayliGht battered black women look grazed

Our double standard as a community stares back at us through the battered eyes of Black women who live under a doubly oppressive system of racism and sexism.
—EWUARE X. OSAYANDE

q. How come abusers say *I love you* the most?

a. we believe them

angelia	*tina*	*latoya*
tjhisha	*janay*	*nene*
dee dee	*rihanna*	*robin*
karrueche	*halle*	*karen*
keke	*christina*	*mariah*
kasandra	*evelyn*	*gramma*
marissa	*emily*	*ma*

me me me me me me me me

i left for school on a tuesday of junior year and never returned. i abducted myself into a safety no one in my world was willing to offer. i freed myself.

a space for the black man who knows no better than

his oppressor

---

even black ***will*** crack if you beat it enough.

in broad dayliGht black girls look grim

she delivers her own eulogy

from the casket

a to-do list

a sort of laundering

things to cleanse the world of in her absence

i ask how she prepared for death

she gives me a list

things to bury with me:

myself

regrets

the asks: if i've ever thought of being with a man

the man (bury him beneath me—as close to the core as possible. that he may burn with no chance of root/rebirth/resurrection).

the truth

the lie

i write about the molestation

but never the rape

bury the rape

i read it

attempt to talk myself out
  of death

out of casket

out of trauma

out of nothing

i don't know

i don't prepare

this is honest—

to myself

i am the opposite

my influence lives beyond
  me

to be some-thing / one

to matter

to resonate

idk

i guess—not to be like a
  person

a dot in the universe—then
  nothing

idk

if it doesn't have an ending,
  i don't need to end it

what are you?

practical

irrelevant

replace—form new
  meaning

it has to be a choice (seed,
  speck, glimmer, spark—
  become a **flame**).

frustrating / to have an end

& keep revisiting

in broad dayliGht black dykes look ground

i used to think there was a dead end at my intersection
i can't unwoman myself
i can't unqueer myself
i can't unmolest or unrape the safety back into my body
i will be black even in death
all of the traffic lights are lit
there's a STOP sign on each corner
above it reads NO OUTLET
Kerrice Lewis is shot and burned alive in the trunk of her
car
this neighborhood of traumas melts together
as the onlooking man wants to know
if i've ever been with one—
a man
the answer is yes, but not in the way he fancies
he straight & hungry for my kind of winding road
and this here is the dead end
i still gotta perform, for him—here
where one avenue say Me Too, and the cross street is
Solidarity
but the next block over ain't Healing
upkeep your own route.
butch, you strong. rugged. like salt-rusted winter road

every corner a speed bump—snow-chained tires over
  your living corpse
you gotta go out the way you came in
naked and weeping

in broad dayliGht kinky black girls look g-spot

If I had a dollar for every time someone said I remind them of their ex when they really meant they wanna fuck me with no strings . . .

Thank God/the music was so loud/whispers echoed our spines/we laughed/right into a memory/the whole time/we danced/you were somebody else's/in front of everyone/in the back/forgot your heartbeat/not/my common sense/got lost/in someone else's back seat/i accepted/your gossip/ nontransferable invite to your pity party/hotel suite/tv was fast and furious/like you/time melted/into sex/sleep/I never undressed/in the sheets as pale/as your ~~skin~~ bitch face/told me everything/i knew was wrong/before you/ no one had ever asked/to kiss me/like i belonged/to me/ you tasted like something/i wanted/'til the sun/tiptoed through the blinds/you mentioned the unmentionable/cast me as the scholar/asked me of the younger/all the reasons/ she can't know/now I'm your secret/the only difference/ between prey and predator/is how wide/you can open/ your mouth

in broad dayliGht black daughters look greedy

My father used to say "the kitchen is closed." When he was there. Even though it had no door. The kitchen was an oasis of leftovers and snacks and juice and red dye number 5. The kitchen closed when he decided we had enough. Food. Drink. Nourishment. When he wasn't there, my mother kept the kitchen open. We were never hungry. Never left to want for anything. But our father. When he wasn't there, she kept the house door open, too.

in broad dayliGht black girls look gleeful

I don't owe anyone more joy than I owe myself.

in broad dayliGht black dykes look good enough to fuck

DeJ Loaf tweets, I'm not a dyke / hoes just love me

A$AP Rocky says, I be fucking broads like I be fucking bored / turn a dyke bitch out have her fucking boys

Kanye says, Heard they'll do anything for a Klondike / I'll do anything for a blonde dyke

Nas says, It's only right that I was born to use mics / and the rhymes that I write is even tougher than dykes

The title of this poem is
"Homophobia vs Homophilia"
or
"How girls kissing girls became a fashionable thing"

Lessons: to the pretty boys with long hair and gold chains that rap about fucking lesbians

there are worse things than being a homosexual
like NOT being a homosexual

like believing your dick is hard enough to fuck a brick wall into stilettos and a miniskirt while still maintaining your masculinity

like how being gay becomes sexy and profitable so long as
you're not

like not understanding the possibility that your dick or any
dick has nothing to do with my sex

dyke: noun

dike[1]

dīk/

1. a long wall or embankment built to prevent flooding
   from the sea

2. a boundary of defense

meaning I am the levee
the arc

and you, sir,
could not possibly handle all this wetness

For God so loved this girl,
he gave his only begotten tongue

A$AP, Get like me,
your girl prolly wish that you would kiss like me
self-trained in the game of such delicacies
So no you will never lick her clit like me

Question: When you fuck a dyke, which one of you is the
daddy?

rhetorical

I had a man tell me once he didn't respect me as a woman
until I opened my mouth

ironic

how I only become his kind of woman once I open my
mouth for him

funny

how an open mouth can be synonymous with bended
knees

sucking off his ego just enough to validate my vagina

this poem is less 10 things I wanna say to a Black Male
Rapper
& more 10 things I need to say to colored dykes who
consider suicide because rap music don't think us human

I tell him, it is not his penile compulsion that compels my
tongue to beat
it is the love of a woman
the body of a woman
that body is mine
it is not built for any man's consumption,
depletion,
or rhyme scheme

It is built for nature
to nurture.
For the record,
we all start out sucking titties
for survival
Some of us are still surviving

in broad dayliGht black dykes look glow

for what it's worth i ain't never wanted to be no man, 'cept
maybe when i gotta pee at the club.
i'm such a fucking lady i can smell my period before it
comes. i knew womanhood before I knew women
i'm *Geraldine*'s granddaughter, which means I'll smack the
shit outta you and make you a mean plate of food.
fuck no I ain't sorry for how I come off. fuck you if you can't
understand it. i'm still gon' reap all these blessings.
making out like a bandit.
i ain't looking for a handout or a handback. fuck your
courts, fuck your fields. when I say reparations i mean
i'm taking my land back. my grandkids' grandkids gon'
draw family trees
with treehouses and hammocks.
i say Black Joy they faces go into panic. like how i know
happiness when they didn't plan it?
forgot I'm the blessing. been praisin' the game like a
reverend. wondered why I'm still stressin'.
i'm *Gayla*'s daughter! watched her make a way of no way
& make dresses.
& teach lessons.
graceful rage & aggression.
raisin' legends.
look at me: Fluorescent!

in broad dayliGht black catcalled dykes look grumpy

catcall II

Ayo, ma!

gucci girl

gimme a smile

gimme a minute

least i aint say gimme a dolla

i love your locs

can you twist mine

i could sit between your legs

i could fit between your legs.

i see you.

i be seein' you.

i'm watching.

i've been watching.

I'd fuck you, with the lights off.

Pussy is pussy.

issa a compliment, bitch.

thassa nigguh.

you a nigguh.

you wanna be a nigguh, so bad.

what? you wanna be a nigguh, ima call you one.

ima treat you like one!

you don't like dick?

you got a dick?

you want some dick?

you need some dick.

fuck with me, you know i got it.

Oh.

You scared?

Yeah.

You scared.

in broad dayliGht black women look grouchy

For within living structures defined by profit, by linear power, by institutional dehumanization, our feelings were not meant to survive. Kept around as unavoidable adjuncts or pleasant pastimes, feelings were meant to kneel to thought as women were expected to kneel to men. But women have survived. As poets. And there are no new pains. We have felt them all already. We have hidden that fact in the same place where we have hidden our power. They surface in our dreams, and it is our dreams that point the way to freedom. Those dreams are made realizable through our poems that give us the strength and courage to see, to feel, to speak, and to dare. —AUDRE LORDE

I tell myself to shut up before i ever utter a word. Before a man inevitably does. Before a lover tells me i'm ruining a moment. I say, shut up, woman. Just write it down. In a text. In a tweet. In a poem. Something easily digestible. To be liked. Shared. Make 'em think you didn't think but just wrote the thing you don't have no business thinking or saying in the first place. I have been invited to perform more than I've been invited to speak. They want the art not the woman behind it. Want the metaphor not the matriarch. I feel like the world feels like I feel like the angry black woman. My senses tell me to fight. They always have. My senses tell me that physical violence is the only mode of protection that has served me. The world tells me this is wrong. I tell my students this is wrong. I want them to believe it. I want me to believe it. In response to this: I study. I write. I share. With the audacity to exist. To speak. To progress. And the men applaud. And the lovers swoon.

in broad dayliGht black bipolar girls look grimy

<u>Things I have been called by professionals:</u>

Bipolar

Compulsive

Catholic

Depressed

Dyslexic

Efficient

Gifted

Impulsive

Obese

Obsessive

I've been baptized twice/washed over/still gay/no choice/
no christian/no cure/girl/no daddy/daughter/no dresses/
jamaican/no accent /girlfriend/no boyfriend/won't tell a lie/
but I'm always swallowing truth/want to run for congress/
but ain't made a move/stand for something even when I'm
sitting/I want to go out/while staying in bed/cuddle without
touching/fuck without loving/love without fighting/I'm
hungry with no appetite/wide awake/with my eyes shut/so
tired/won't sleep/bathed/still dirty/like my sloppy neat/I
like my neat never/smile when I'm angry/cry when I'm
happy/spend what I don't have/living when I want to die/

trying to die when I'm supposed to live/I'm the strongest woman you know/in her weakest moment/I'm allergic to peanuts and have been stabbed with an EpiPen/swallowed 30 times the prescribed amount of antidepressants stood smiling over my weeping almost dead body/my mother calls me fearless/my father doesn't call/built by a broken home/the only thing I've ever been afraid of is my lack of fear/my emotions are an 18-wheeler in rush hour/if home is where the heart is I owe back rent to my own chest/I never knew how or forgot along the way to wash the dishes put the pain in the dryer/I'm only breathing because the enemy wants me dead/turned my back on the devil to advocate for someone who actually needs it/I walked away from the cross to have a Godson named Lucifer and he's a fucking angel/our hugs are crowbars and a part of me is broken into/choosing to learn/to love another good boy who will grow into whatever he chooses/I had to choose me/choose to live/there's a chance he'll need my kind of monster to scare away the bad & I'll be ready & never alone/every best friend I've ever had is writing these poems with my hands/so I'll never have to work again/for now death is behind the back of my mind LIVE scrolls LED bright across the marquee of my eyelids/I'm the rolling credits after a sunset/my memories are deleted scenes/I've held a pistol to my head but never brought one home/the only shotgun in my possession is a passenger seat aimed at anyone down to ride for me the clip is endless/& the door is unlocked

in broad dayliGht black victims looked gagged

q. What are the consequences of silence?

a.

silence is a lynching
of things the world already knows about you
but still
needs to choke from your throat

silence is a cloak
draped over a body
of lies
has the world thinking you are safe//whole
something worth listening to
because everything is
the truth
once you believe it

silence is not just deadly
but the weapon itself
left at the scene of the crime
used to extinguish
generations
of black mental health issues
because black people don't have

time for exhaustion//depression
we will do our work//massa's work//
& still have time
to be slaves to our own
trauma

silence is blinding
the reason i look for children
the way no one looked for me
is deafening
how no one heard my cries for help
or cries to sleep
impenetrable
how we cannot break
through
my depression

The consequences of silence will leave me lying in traffic
on 42nd Street
Believing the only imprint i'll have on the world is what's
left after the cars stampede over my body

is a drug
i was so strung out
no one knew i wished to die

until I had a stomach full of pills
& when i woke up
still trapped on this bridge
between heaven & hell
silence rendered me speechless
i had no song to sing
silence is no apology
no thank you
my mother,
didn't know
how to
welcome me to the
world a second time

pessimism is trying to kill myself
optimism is living afterward

i have silence beaten into my body
i exist in this constant state of rage
when my hands don't know
when my mouth can handle it

and so sometimes my tongue
swings before my fist do
& vice versa
& sometimes they wild out
at the same ga'damn time

no one wants to be a victim out of love
they do it out of threat
of whip
fist
gun
shame

silence does not make a victim out of me
predators do
silence means i never tell my mother
i was molested
because he is family
because he is bigger than me
because i should have known better

silence means i don't tell my friends i was abused
because she was a woman
because she wasn't bigger than me
because i should have known better

i say nothing
because defending myself is
seen as an attack to my attacker
i say nothing because doing nothing is
seen as an attack on myself

i use silence for safety

they think me strong
think I can take it
because I've been witness
to my own murder
& still ain't said shit

i am teaching myself
how to peel back the layers of silence
when the only undressing
i've known has been
in front of those who never deserved
to see

silence is not always a choice
it can be
a protest
the thin line
between danger
& safety

saying nothing
doesn't mean everything's all right
saying nothing can mean everything
is all wrong
but it doesn't make it any less real

saying nothing means look at me

close

& hard

my whole body

is a language—

& i'm begging you

learn it

homage to dyke girls with gap-tooth smiles

You still gay no matter how much you smile
straighten your hair
curve your spine
Your butch more visible than your black sometime.

You know,
your smile a gateway to safety
The beginning of your happiness
An interstice for grief and greed to slip in
Holy to be spit out

You know,
if there is a god
he got some 'splainin to do

I know,
if there is a god she
black—tired of yo shit
& ain't 'splainin a ga'damn thing

That's why you got this crevice

behind your lips

So even when you breathe

the truth come seeping through like a whistle.

in broad dayliGht black mfa candidates look glamorous

or, the glamour of a systematically oppressive MFA program

or, questions I asked my future self when the future was my impeding breath:

1. Can you breathe?
2. Who saved you?
3. What is the urgency in your writing and who are you going to save if not yourself?
4. Sometimes the future is tomorrow, are you ready?
5. How much longer will you wait to talk about the things you have chosen to write?
6. Who will care?
7. Are you willing to die for this?
8. Is it possible to promote your own blackness in the presence of antiblackness?
9. Is any of this worth retraumatizing yourself?
10. Will any of it ever set you free?

The first thing she said to me after the diagnosis was that I had every right to be bipolar. She grabbed me by the face right here on this campus and made me feel one. There's no way for a black woman to exist and persist in this world without experiencing the extreme of every high and low it has to offer. I agree, I am everything they say I am. I also know that I am none of these things. That itself is a huge knot in my throat. My gall to disagree is the crime that justifies my end. It never sounds like a lynching until the rope snaps. Until the trachea submits and the eyes roll home. Patriot and patriarchy be one and the same in the classroom, where a queer black woman mistakenly breathes a breath that no man sanctioned. Here, he is law and fuckboy, passed and passing as some creed we must abide. He is well traveled but hunts here for sport. (me). Here, I am always something different. One thing before the other. Right now it's black. Right now it's woman. Right now it's queer. Right now it still does not matter. (to him). My intersection is just another crossroad. A red light he will surely run—with no regard. The classroom is his crash site. So many bystanders. So much rubbernecking and still no one calls for help. Just watch him burn in his own racial insecurity. My tinsel-wrapped throat, all sparkly and constricted, dangles high from an oak in the distance. My eyes will never be as bright as his headlights. My cries never as loud as the gridlocked horns. My body never as wrecked as the cars. The rope snaps. The knot tightens. The gasping is drowned out by the sirens. Soon, he will be safe again. Blanketed by the warmth of some emergency professional or bro or mansplaining woman. I'll have choked down everything I meant to say in the name of feminism or blackness for the sake of existing. Waiting for the rope and gravity and my own resistance to do me in.

in broad dayliGht black dykes look go

the bible be a fascinatin' book of fiction.
got all kinds of tricks & schemes & wonder

how folk still buy it. live by it. die by it.
i read them tales in there.

tall'a than that tree as smart as all get out
& that god fella, him think dyin' a metaphor.

say you git what you git & don't throw no fit.
like the ground ca' just swallow a gurl.

his world gon' wish away.
& i git it, that gumption get ya cursed.

but eve. eve aint ne'er wanna be no s*n.
not on this earth, dirt & damned, or any.

every gurl in there got some flaw. mostly
make it look like she chasin' some man to the end

of the world. when she always only eva been chasin'
daylight.

& he still convinced the s*n come up just to hear him crow.
them stories as crooked as a barrel of snakes.

most'a it seem like just pickin'.
i reckon the only time a man come first is . . .

awww, don' pay me no nevamind. i'm always fussin' on
sum'n. startin' arguments in a empty house.

just wonder, in all them stories, if a period make a page
dirty like it do a woman?

well, i'm fixin' to have my own genesis & there shall be no
more curse & no more night & we be first & last.

call it blasphemy, but dammit this time the black girl come
home!!

this time the black girl come home.
yeh, that's it. this time the black girl go home.

in broad dayliGht black sisters look glass

the word faggot
shoots off
my brother's
tongue
more often
than good morning

he doesn't think it
offends me
he doesn't believe
the barrel of his
voice could hold
the bullet that
would call me
cadaver

i say,
when a stranger
calls
me a black
dyke
nigga
bitch
i don't know
where to insert

comma

or

know which name

does the least

damage

because

that's the one i'll

turn

into compliment

or think it a

blessing

they left me alive

enough

to hear it

i must be lucky

men offer to let

me suck their

dicks more often

than straight

women

an honor

some think their

wives

too clean for

they offer to save
me
make me walk
crooked
fuck me straight
be the daddy
i ain't have
ain't want
gon' show me
what I been
missing

what I'm supposed
to do
when a stranger
wish me dead?

his heart
beats in his throat
and he says
i'll rip out the
tongue
of any
motherfucker that
would

i swallow and say,
start with yours

in broad dayliGht black dykes look gomorrah

megaphone Jesus says I am the abomination

when I pass his tribe on 149

With his Israelite robe and sparkly headdress

said my denim jeans were ungodly.

One minute I come from Kings

The next I'm the devil's plaything

both royalty and meant to bow

to those that won't rise for me

at least not in my time of need

at least not if I don't bend knee

and that's just it

I was Nubian a moment ago, y'all

Right up until i ain't wanna guzzle his kids

even tho I'm so good at doing what i don't want

like making men erect

but can't make a man erect a statue

in my honor

fuckable until proven dick free

He ain't even tryna know my name

Let alone say it

His god and mine suffer a language barrier

How you create your own sect

and still manage to worship a god that's more involved in
my sex than my safety

How you preaching the word of your lord

and cussing me in the name of your crotch
Oh yeah,
you believe the seed comes from the father?
in Hebrew seed is Zephra
which translates to semen.
is that what you spittin?
or you been swallowing so long you don't know whose shit
you eating?
Flex, then!
Oh, you think I'm scared?
Nigga I crossed the grand concourse without the light
I still love Kanye
I still got white friends
I've been to hell
Trapped inside my own mouth
a scorching of things I was afraid to say aloud
You think calling
me an abomination makes me forget you still wanna fuck
me?
silence a truth, erase a fault.
do you hear church bell sirens?
ordain me
a wannabe
man hater
man herself
Name me anything but beautiful.
first you pray I'll call

then you'll call me prey
Today, I renounce my god
Like Peter
Like Judas
Like Longinus
I renounce my Black
Like OJ
Like Tiger
Like Raven
Today I'm just a vessel
that eats pussy
Even then, someone wants me dead
in the name of the father
who reigns when he pleases
& here I go with the audacity to keep on living
I'm into going against the grain
Lord knows I want you to stay
Pray a roof over your head
Pray every Dylann Roof away from NYCHA
that your brother remains your keeper
Wish your flesh be armor
I'll be miscreant
Evildoer
the darkness

and still be the baddest bitch in the plaza

in broad dayliGht black queer femmes look gala

issa celebration

lace front flyin'

locs whippin'

that bass beating down to the city of yo' sole

ain't no nerve in yo' body sleep

issa ball

have a ball

you the honoree

you made it!

at least tonight

the bullshit gon' have try again another day

cuz you here.

in broad dayliGht black stars look like gyrochronology

astronomers can decipher the age of a star by their spin
rate

the scientific term for this is gyrochronology

Gyros meaning rotation

Chronos meaning age

Logos meaning study

A study of age through rotation

my first tattoo was a star

a branding of sorts

something to tell my body apart from the others

My flesh akin to ruin

akin to loss

the study of age through rotation

a preteen

a toy

a gun

a boy

a bullet

a barrel

a trigger

a finger

a cell

a trash bag

a backyard

a playground

a car

my resolve

every nigga is a star

meant for shooting

not for target.

q. how do you tell the age of a dead body?

a. you check for blackness. if no blackness the body will still be breathing.
b. you pluck a star from its mouth.
c. the more massive the star, the faster it burns up its fuel supply, and the shorter its life.
d. the most massive stars can burn out before they finish high school.

corpses in crosswalks

rising to the hudson surface

swinging from trees

you can't metaphor modern-day lynchings

when there are actually modern-day lynchings

bodies buried beneath me whisper run

to my ankles between cackles

I am always weeping

my love asks why i cry at night.

Like the stars,

my tears are most visible in the dark.

in broad dayliGht black dykes look grilled

my feminism is visible

big breasted

smart mouthed

often discounted

& ignored

always wearing shades or throwing it

got bottom grillz

two master's degrees

is Teyana Taylor in that Kanye video

dressed like Queen Latifah in *Set It Off*

ain't woman enough for the straight ones

ain't man enough for the gay ones

sags sometimes when I don't wear a belt

shops in men's departments.

hard

but ain't bullet proof

is proof of the bullet

my feminism is Jesus

the real one

the black one

with locs

on the cross

no the ankh

crucified

broken free

cupping the world on its bare shoulders

can carry a baby

but ain't too sure about pushing it out

my feminism is mother

is a motherfucker

wish a motherfucker would

might smile at you but not for you

will grab trump by his pussy

even though he's all asshole

gets catcalled

and called dog

by women who hate how masculine my feminism is

it don't make women loyal

don't make them stable

or stay

gets cheated on

& called too feminine

for having feelings about it

my feminism is exhausted

of your expectations

& being judged

& being denied

& explaining its own femininity

in broad dayliGht black abuse victims look gone

from the one who left

Used to say I been beaten

but I'm still here

fight ain't over

I never died

The trauma did

"No one is to approach any close relative to have sexual relations." Leviticus 18:6

he said it was a nightmare

he said it was a nervous tic

he said it was a game

he never said I couldn't tell

I think,   that's why I didn't

something in me knew

this was **not**

good news

worth sharing

so i swallowed it & him

Used to say I been beaten

but I'm still here

fight ain't over

I never died

The trauma did

but was born again

of another man's mouth

"Do not envy a violent man or choose any of his ways."

Proverbs 3:31

he said you are

your mother's

daughter

but you are my mistake

said if you didn't turn around

the shoe would have hit your head

not split your lip

said if you ever tell a soul

you will need more than a few stitches

so i tucked this deep

Used to say I been beaten

but I'm still here

fight ain't over

I never died

The trauma did

but was born again of

another woman's fist

"Beloved, do not avenge yourselves, but rather give place to wrath; for it is written, 'Vengeance is Mine, I will repay,' says the Lord." Romans 12:19

she said i asked for it
she said i made her
she said it wouldn't be abuse
if I would just fight back
said the bruises would fade
but the love would grow stronger
she said i just happen to be around
at her worst times
she said playing the victim only makes her hit harder
she said no one in love
should have to beg for sex
she said this isn't kidnapping
I just gotta get through her if I wanna leave
so i stayed

I used to say I been beaten
but I'm still here
therapist on speed dial
41 empty pill bottles later
sleepless nights turned morning
countless exhales

trauma will never have

as many revivals

as triumph

"The Spirit of the Lord GOD is upon Me, because the LORD has anointed Me to preach good tidings to the poor; He has sent Me to heal the brokenhearted, to proclaim liberty to the captives, and the opening of the prison to those who are bound." Isaiah 61:1

Victory is the moment I looked my father in the eye and didn't swing

Victory is the moment I looked my ex in the eye and didn't jump

Victory is the moment I looked my molester in the eye

and didn't shoot

Victory is the moment I look myself in the eye

& lived

& loved

blessed are the wicked

for they shall inherit

the courage to love

bloodlessly

Blessed are the captive

for they shall inherit

the courage to escape

still breathing

i

walked free

a chance to live again

the difference between death

& survival

how you can dance

at your own grave site

the beaten are where they always were

trying to fight/fuck their rage out of the good around them

they keep checking the tomb for my remains

& each time I am gone

There's a decade of resurrection Sundays

buried underneath my tongue

i am the good news

consider me the burning bush

you damn right I'm on fire

I've been carrying the sun on my spine

intending to light the way

for the ones who stayed

in broad dayliGht black thrivers look growth

or, well-wishes from the other side

May you learn forgiveness is the whisper in a seashell
awaiting your ear
you have bloomed backwards many a season
still expected to be vase ready
you prickly and painful
May you know there are hands crafted to carry bouquets
of you
You burst of blooming burst of Blackness
May you know light spills like blud and both will lead you
somewhere
someone will need your goodness for pollination
someone will feed on you
May you be enough to nourish
and still be good enough to you
every tree falls when it's ready to live differently
I am worth more than a metaphor for trauma
painted in florals and fruit, but gardens are beautiful
and I've seen some survive the brutal of winter.

The thing is,
I'm healing.

in broad dayliGht black moms look swollen gland

or, Langston Hughes tells you of your mother's cancer 2 months before her 65th birthday

Sensing death,
The buzzards gather
—LANGSTON HUGHES, "DYING BEAST"

when quality health is in vogue
& the last bite of the ghetto is devoured
on the purple checkout line
at the trader joe's that replaced the homeless shelter
where they always got a story about someone they used to
  know
where if people suffered, they suffered in beautiful language
you learn sometimes a body is just too fine.
there was a buyout & most folks copped out
but not yo' mama.
worked 'til the shelter turned to rubble.
rubble turn to rinky-dink restaurant.

that's what cancer does, gentrifies.
wraps up a body.
juice it 'til crust & bald.
you busy wondering what the blues will bring

cuz you was always planning to die
first—
& now she got cells growing uncontrollably
that won't die
& ain't no hope in hopin' she make it through
& who all gon' care for you when she gone
home?
when the rent due
ya shorty wildin'
ya calories addin' up
& you six weeks into the dollar menu
and the doctor say diabetes got a borderline
& you seekin' asylum in a food desert.

you remember you don't visit cemeteries
so when it's time for you to say goodbye
you better say it well
you better say it loud
you remember
that poison is gentrifying your mother's body
if you tryna snuggle up in yours you can't leave room
for vacancies or intruders
you remember the hood as an undying beast
while the vultures surround
malignant mall & matinee w/ mimosas

and just like they did your hood
they start taking shit out of her body
they start putting shit into her body
radioactive chips that prevent her from speaking
for the meantime, they say.
for the better, they say.

the cancer is gone, for now.
she is home, for now.
a stomach demolished.
a thyroid removed.
a death deferred.
& you still ain't made plans.
you gotta remember, now
the clock is ticking
ain't no coming back from living, again.

in broad dayliGht black lovers look guest

I think love is a hotel room

everything used

but new

I arrive with arms full of gifts

The most precious wrapped

inside of my chest

the lampshades bow and the tv won't even look at me

I am never more useless

than in the arms of a woman

who will check out

before i even know the sun has risen

I keep falling for the same women

dying or dead

with hearts on

do not deserve

I know I am no god

I know nothing of forgiveness

I carry such a sadness

for all the sorries I've never received

to know I cannot hold you close

to know I cannot forgive

is to know you are no longer with me

there are no crossroads

no latent reunion

You had no desire to be a lover

we, a casualty of human nature

sometimes love is letting you die

do not disturb

There must be a way to remind myself

this bed

is not a casket

oh, lucky you

who gets to be spirit

I'm forced to remain human

But we are both daughters

to someone

//a glimpse//

of everything that is good

and just

and right

We right

& write
until the world knows of this unspeakable tenderness & our
  undeserving need
to be known as legacies
as daughters
of daughters
who may beget daughters

My pastor once told me,
in prayer
I have to use the only words that work
today it's fuck
today it's die
tomorrow it may be live or love or or or
either way you will not respond

I am learning my posture of worship is my head thrown
  back
two middle fingers in the air
screaming fuck the unworthy

There are things that I've said that did not sound godly
there are places I have been that look nothing like heaven
I have been begging a deafened lord to write messages
  over your heart

but your funeral is not my burden

love is no religion

this is no church

it's just this hotel room

where—like me,

everything is used

but seemingly new

we are significant and other

the door is calling

& it's time

to check out

What are the conditions of your freedom?

DYKE DYKE DYKE DYKE DYKE DYKE DYKE DYKE DYKE DYKE
DYKE DYKE DYKE DYKE DYKE DYKE DYKE DYKE DYKE DYKE
DYKE DYKE DYKE DYKE DYKE DYKE DYKE DYKE DYKE DYKE
DYKE DYKE DYKE DYKE DYKE DYKE DYKE DYKE DYKE DYKE
DYKE DYKE DYKE DYKE DYKE DYKE DYKE DYKE DYKE DYKE
DYKE DYKE DYKE DYKE DYKE DYKE DYKE DYKE DYKE DYKE
DYKE DYKE DYKE DYKE DYKE DYKE DYKE DYKE DYKE DYKE
DYKE DYKE DYKE DYKE DYKE DYKE DYKE DYKE DYKE DYKE
DYKE DYKE DYKE DYKE DYKE DYKE DYKE DYKE DYKE DYKE
DYKE DYKE DYKE DYKE DYKE DYKE DYKE DYKE DYKE DYKE
DYKE DYKE DYKE DYKE DYKE DYKE DYKE DYKE DYKE DYKE
DYKE DYKE DYKE DYKE DYKE DYKE DYKE DYKE DYKE DYKE
DYKE DYKE DYKE DYKE DYKE DYKE DYKE DYKE DYKE DYKE
DYKE DYKE DYKE DYKE DYKE DYKE DYKE DYKE DYKE DYKE
DYKE DYKE DYKE DYKE DYKE DYKE DYKE DYKE DYKE DYKE
DYKE DYKE DYKE DYKE DYKE DYKE DYKE DYKE DYKE DYKE
DYKE DYKE DYKE DYKE DYKE DYKE DYKE DYKE DYKE DYKE
DYKE DYKE DYKE DYKE DYKE DYKE DYKE DYKE DYKE DYKE
DYKE DYKE DYKE DYKE DYKE DYKE DYKE DYKE DYKE DYKE
DYKE DYKE DYKE DYKE DYKE DYKE DYKE DYKE DYKE DYKE
DYKE DYKE DYKE DYKE DYKE DYKE DYKE DYKE DYKE DYKE
DYKE DYKE DYKE DYKE DYKE DYKE DYKE DYKE DYKE DYKE
DYKE DYKE DYKE DYKE DYKE DYKE DYKE DYKE DYKE DYKE
DYKE DYKE DYKE DYKE DYKE DYKE DYKE DYKE DYKE DYKE
DYKE DYKE DYKE DYKE DYKE DYKE DYKE DYKE DYKE DYKE
DYKE DYKE DYKE DYKE DYKE DYKE DYKE DYKE DYKE DYKE
DYKE DYKE DYKE DYKE DYKE DYKE DYKE DYKE DYKE DYKE
DYKE DYKE DYKE DYKE DYKE DYKE DYKE DYKE DYKE DYKE
DYKE DYKE DYKE DYKE DYKE DYKE DYKE DYKE DYKE DYKE
DYKE DYKE DYKE DYKE DYKE DYKE DYKE DYKE DYKE DYKE
DYKE DYKE DYKE DYKE DYKE DYKE DYKE DYKE DYKE DYKE
DYKE DYKE DYKE DYKE DYKE DYKE DYKE DYKE DYKE DYKE
DYKE DYKE DYKE DYKE DYKE DYKE DYKE DYKE DYKE DYKE
DYKE DYKE DYKE DYKE DYKE DYKE DYKE DYKE DYKE DYKE
DYKE DYKE DYKE DYKE DYKE DYKE DYKE DYKE DYKE DYKE
DYKE DYKE DYKE DYKE DYKE DYKE DYKE DYKE DYKE DYKE

acknowledgments

Wooo! If it wasn't for the Bronx, this Black girl prolly never would be writin' poems. Shout out to where I'm from. Uptown Baby, Uptown Baby!

Sincere gratitude to Danny Vazquez and the entire team at MCD / Farrar, Straus and Giroux for believing, and for pushing and fighting for this project to see the light of day.

The women in my family are Gz. All of my love and thanks to Grandma Geraldine, whose words I grew up on & continue to live by. You were the wisest and most stubborn woman the world had to offer.

Ma & Aunty, y'all set the bar high for the woman I always knew I needed to be. Each of you made it possible for me to exist, and there aren't enough words in all the poems in all the world to amass the supernatural powers each of you possess.

To my father, for everything that you are and for all of the things that you are not.

To my siblings: Thank you for lending me your lives. I am the greatest parts of each of you. I learned how powerful I am by watching you all survive.

Incredible thanks to the next gen & the reasons I grind the

hardest: Domo, Larry, Shonyay, Miana, Sierra, Ihsiah, Chancy V., Joseph, Sharissa, Malcolm, Prynce, Autumn, Amazeyn, Bricyn, Alexander, Ariceli, Amari.

Mad love to my Uncle Lyle & the Walford family & the Moody family & the Claffee families & the White family & the Millender family for sitting on the floors of venues way back when every poem rhymed, for coming to the plays & the documentaries, for buying the books, and for every moment you checked for me.

The fiercest: Mahogany L. Browne, you've been an anchor and armor since the moment we connected. Seester, for picking me up off of the floor (literally), every time. Jive Poetic, you've given me more than enough encouragement to believe in myself.[2] Whitney Greenaway for reading every version of this manuscript and learning every version of me.

To Joslyn & Marlene & Kevin & Matthew & Ampi & Meela & Will for lasting love and friendship that taught me the magic of platonic intimacy. The Alston, Rivas & Martinez families, y'all have been here from the beginning and you're still here.

Eddie, my first boyfriend, you are now, and forever will be, a true love of my life.

Melody, we started out as close friends and are now family forever. #FreeNene 'til we say it backward!

To Isabel & the Rodriguez family, for your constant love and support. Thank you for LJ, he's the purest and warmest love.

Noel, my brother and business partner, we're basically married.

Saquayah, I've never felt more supported than when I'm on your couch with a warm meal and some iced TP.

Tay, you are always ready to love and super eager to learn. Thank you for showing up.

Charlie Poems! You've been a rock even when you weren't sturdy.

Mel, in the last moments of this, you swooped in and gave the most necessary push. Shout out to G*D for the kind of love few think is possible.

My endless love to the legendary artists and activists of Urban Word NYC. Sofia, Adam, Shanelle, Marissa, Sergio, Jose, MJ, Michael & ALL MY CHILDREN (Slam Dad loves you). Y'all have supported me and contributed to my growth as an artist and human in immeasurable ways.

To the poets and writers who have pushed my pen: Amyra Leon, Katherine George, Steven Willis, Crystal Valentine, Christopher Shawn, Michael Lilley, Anthony McPherson, Paul Tran, Eboni Hogan, Imani Davis, Chelsea Alison, Zubaida Bello, Aaliyah Daniels, Nathaniel Swanson, Demetria Mack, Camryn Bruno, William Lohier, Danez Smith, sam sax, Paragraph, Jamie Lewis, Ebony Stewart (Dear Heart), Jon Sands, Amir Safi, Saraciea Fennell (you trusted my mouth and my heart), Venessa Marco, Edwin Bodney (& Myko), Tre G., Shihan Van Clief, Barbara Fant, Team Feels (Tariq Luthun, Jose Soto, RJ Walker), J.David Ockunzzi (you have the purest heart), Rebecca Gonzales (trampoline), Tongo Eisen-Martin, Joseph Sun Hernandez, Charlie Poems, Danny Matos, Thomas Fucaloro, Rob V., Chulisi, AR Garcia, Angy Abreu, Deria Matthews, Aarushi Agni, Caelan Nardone, Sharifa Rhodes-Pitts, and the countless others who have lifted, soothed, and endured me as I am, through morality and flaws.

Dear reader: I am grateful for you & your attention. Because of you this book lives another day.